323·4

This book is ⁺
the ¹

He had a Dream

He had a Dream

Martin Luther King, Jr., and the Civil Rights Movement

by Flip Schulke

Designed by Robert S. Nemser

W · W · Norton & Company   New York · London

Acknowledgments

This documentary photography book could not be done without the gifts of both time and creativity of many people. I am extremely grateful to James Mairs, my editor at W. W. Norton & Company, for his suggestions, patience, confidence, and especially his persistence in all aspects of this book. His continued interest, compassion, and knowledge of civil rights history is unsurpassed. Thanks also to his associate, Tabitha Griffin, who has been a real joy to work with.

Many thanks to my book designer, Robert Nemser. After working on three Martin Luther King, Jr., books together, Bob is one of a kind. An historian, he understands the civil rights movement and has the rare ability to select photographs of mine that I have never payed attention to. He has opened my eyes so many times.

A book containing photographs is only as good as the man or woman in the darkroom who prints my negatives as I want them (and often finds ways to make the prints better than I could possibly imagine). My heartfelt thanks to Ricki Troiano, Wolfram Kloetz, Vernon Sigl, and Jorge Figueroa of Modernage Custom Labs in New York; Joe Lucinian, Paul Plyler, and Skip Thomson of Thomson Photo Lab in Coral Gables, Florida; Jim Heading of National Camera in West Palm Beach; and Matthew Wynd and Steve Harley of American Images (CD-ROM scanning) in Rochester, New York.

My appreciation to Howard Chapnick of Black Star Picture Agency, for encouraging photography of the civil rights struggle. Thanks are also due to Herbert Nipson, former editor, and John H. Johnson, publisher of *Jet* and *Ebony* magazines, whose assignments introduced me to Dr. King.

My deepest thanks to those in the southern civil rights movement who have helped me after the photographs were taken, including: Reverend C. T. Vivian, Octavia Vivian, Reverend Hosea Williams, Reverend Ralph Abernathy, Representative Walter Fauntroy, Andrew Young, Julian Bond, Dr. Joseph Lowery, Representative John Lewis, Burke Marshall, and Bruce Keys of the Martin Luther King, Jr., Center for Nonviolent Social Change in Atlanta, Georgia. Thanks also to Matt Herron, photojournalist. To all the unsung heroes of the SCLC, NAACP, CORE, Urban League, SNCC, and Mississippi Summer Project, whose names I don't know, thank you for educating me in the ways of the South.

To the reporters working for *Life* magazine during that era whose thankless task was to write the captions and stories to my photographs, I shall always remember our days together fondly. Thank you Mike Durham, Reg Bragonier, Ed Reingold, Bob Fellows, Wayne Warga, David Nivin, Don Underwood, Hal Wingo, Mike Silva, Miguel Acoca, Ron Bailey, Rudy Cheminski, Miami Bureau Chiefs, Dick Billings, and Hank Suydam, and Shana Alexander, who wrote the best story to come out of the marches at Selma, Alabama. Thanks to the memory of Bill Lyons of UPI, and Jim Boudier of AP, with whom I traded film and "secret" information unbeknownst to all of our publications. I will always treasure the closeness between southern civil rights photographers.

Special thanks to the Trenton State College Computer Graphics Lab, Ruane Miller, Richard Rose, and Rochelle Kaiden. My deepest thanks to Gary Truman, Joe Toreno, Dave, Nancy, and Leslie Harrington, who saved the King negatives from the hurricane. A toast to Jennifer Lyons of the Joan Daves Agency—you really care. Champagne for Starling Lawrence of W. W. Norton, who started it all.

Finally, my deepest affection and appreciation to Coretta Scott King, who has carried on King's philosophy through the center which she founded—the Martin Luther King, Jr., Center for Nonviolent Social Change—so ably assisted by Yoki, Marty, Dexter, and Bunny. As your father looks down on you all continuing his work, he must be very proud.

Printed in Italy by Arnoldo Mondadori Editore, Verona, Italy

The text of this book is composed in Bookman with the display set in Bookman Bold

Book design and composition by Robert S. Nemser

Manufacturing by Arnoldo Mondadori Editore, Verona, Italy

Library of Congress Cataloging-in-Publication Data
Schulke, Flip.
    He had a dream: Martin Luther King, Jr., and the civil rights movement
  / Flip Schulke; designed by Robert S. Nemser.
        p. cm.

    1. King, Martin Luther, Jr., 1929-1968—Pictorial works. 2. Afro-
  Americans—Civil rights—Pictorial works. 3. Civil rights movements—
  United States—History—20th century—Pictorial works.
  I. Title.
  E 185.97.K5S37 1995
  323'.092—dc20   94-27506
      ISBN 0-393-03729-0
      ISBN 0-393-31264-X (pbk.)

W. W. Norton & Company, Inc., 500 Fifth Avenue, New York, N.Y. 10110

W. W. Norton & Company Ltd., 10 Coptic Street, London WC1A 1PU

1 2 3 4 5 6 7 8 9 0

Dedication

To Donna Lee Schulke, whose nurturing encouragement brought forth many deeply hidden memories, and to Macalester College in St. Paul, Minnesota, where I learned to understand and care for civil rights for all people.

"We see men as Jews or Gentiles, Catholics or Protestants, Chinese or Americans, Negroes or Whites. We fail to think of them as fellow human beings made from the same basic stuff as we, molded in the same divine image."
—Martin Luther King, Jr.

Contents

Hero. The dictionary describes a hero as: 1. A man in mythology and legend celebrated for his strength and bold exploits. 2. A man noted for his special achievements.

My heroes growing up varied from Abraham Lincoln, Charles Lindbergh, General Dwight D. Eisenhower, to Batman. I was awed by their accomplishments and fearlessness. I read about them in books, newspapers, and comics. But I have been lucky enough to have known a true hero—Reverend Martin Luther King, Jr. Though his life was tragically cut short, he shook the generation in which he lived and he continues to affect and inspire lives today.

As Penelope McPhee and I stated in Martin Luther King, Jr.: A Documentary . . . Montgomery to Memphis: "The facts of King's life are clear . . . that which he said was wrong has been proven wrong, and that which he believed was right has been proven right. The years have demonstrated that the strategies and philosophies in the black movement which King found morally offensive were also ineffective." Dr. King, in a January 1965 interview in Playboy magazine, spoke of Malcolm X and the Black Muslims: "I totally disagree with many of his [Malcolm X] political and philosophical views. . . . I have often wished he would talk less of violence, because violence is not going to solve our problem. And in his litany of articulating the despair of the Negro without offering any positive, creative alternative, I feel that Malcolm has done himself and our people a disservice." As far as I know, this is the only public statement Dr. King ever made about Malcolm X. One month later, in February 1965, Malcolm X was murdered while speaking to his new group, the Organization of Afro-American Unity. It is interesting to note that before his death, Malcolm X had indeed begun to change many of his previously held views about violence.

Dr. King believed in the total political and economic integration of all races and creeds. His philosophy of nonviolent civil action prompted the enfranchisement of Afro-Americans in the South and across the nation. Since that time, as memories dim and people from that era pass on, too much of that history is being revised and homogenized. We now live in an age of cynicism. Our responses to the strength, bold exploits, and special achievements of men and women today have changed. Though I understand that new times warrant different approaches to racial problems, I want to stress what Dr. King's actions and philosophy did at that time in the 1960s. Dr. King did not wait for change and evolution to occur naturally. He perpetrated it. He incited evolution. His greatness was his ability to analyze and attack the roots of an issue. He forced people to alter deeply ingrained attitudes, social customs, and convictions—not merely to change laws. And he did this by teaching Gandhi's principles of nonviolent direct action. Perhaps these methods will not help the cause of racial injustice and prejudice now or in the future, but it did turn the tide, single-handedly, in the 1960s.

This book is my own personal view, seen through the lens of my heart, mind, and camera. It is about a particular time in history. A time I witnessed, participated in, and documented. I was biased. There are not "two sides" to segregation. There is no justification for the oppression of a people. Much of the time, one can recognize these biases and keep them from tainting journalistic reports. But occasionally, events do conflict with personal moral beliefs and at these moments, I follow the dictates of my conscience. I photographed events in Dr. King's life, and the racial struggles of the 1960s, with a deep belief in Dr. King's ideas.

Dr. King greatly expanded my knowledge and awareness, and the photographs in this book reflect what I gained from knowing him. One of America's most highly respected photojournalists, W. Eugene Smith, said that photography is a small voice. I agree with him. Journalistic photographs in themselves can't inform the viewer completely; an explanation is necessary. But a photograph does have the power to elicit from the viewer the need to know more about the subject matter. When I show my southern civil rights photographs to students, whether in grade schools or in colleges, I receive hundreds of de-

mands to "tell us more" about those times. The visual is immediate and excites quickly, and it is my hope that these photographs will create a desire within the viewer to know more about Dr. King. (My archive of over 11,000 photographs will be housed at Macalester College Library in St. Paul, Minnesota, both in original film and CD-ROM disc form, to be made available to students of all ages. Photojournalist David Douglas Duncan taught me the importance of preserving these moments of history—a practice that has been reinforced by Hurricane Andrew, which nearly destroyed the original negatives and color slides.)

Dr. King believed in the essential goodness of humankind. His concern was for the rights of Afro-Americans, but it was also for the rights of women, the poor, and for all the disadvantaged. He showed us a way. He showed us that people of good will can prevail against all odds, if we only try in our own circle of influence, whether it be small or large. In the words of Father James Keller: It is better to light one candle than to curse the darkness.

I first met Dr. Martin Luther King, Jr., on an assignment for *Ebony* magazine during February 1958. He was twenty-nine years old, and I was twenty-eight. Though white, I had been shooting for *Ebony* and *Jet* magazines in the deep South since 1956. During the 1950s, it became quite difficult for a black photographer from Chicago, where *Ebony* and *Jet* magazines were located, to fulfill assignments in the lower southern states because of harassment in many of the smaller towns.

I had become interested in racial problems while attending Macalester College in my home state of Minnesota. Senator Hubert H. Humphrey had instigated the original plank supporting the integration of U.S. public schools at the Democratic National Convention in 1948, and had taught at Macalester before he was elected mayor of Minneapolis, and then U.S. senator. When I moved to Miami in the early 1950s, I was eager and well situated to be an "undercover" photographer for the black publications of Johnson Publishing Company. My first assignments, however, were not racial confrontation stories. Instead, they were on black sports figures, successful black business people, pre-Castro Cuba, and the Bahamas.

In February of 1958, I was assigned to photograph the Reverend Martin Luther King, Jr., at a fund-raising rally held in a downtown Miami Baptist church. I had followed Dr. King in the news during the Montgomery, Alabama, bus boycott in 1955 and 1956 and knew of his advocacy of Gandhi's nonviolent techniques in the overturning of segregation on city buses there.

As I listened to his speech about the problems of the Negro in the United States and in the South, questions formed in my mind. After the rally was over and I had finished photographing, I went up to Dr. King and posed some of the questions to him. He asked me to come with him to the house of a local Miami minister, where he was staying for the night. After all the other guests had left, we sat down to an all-night session discussing civil rights problems. Dr. King was one year older than I was, and though he had a Ph.D., he treated me as a peer.

Our conversation came around to the press and photo coverage of news events. He said that very little of what his new group, the Southern Christian Leadership Conference (SCLC), was involved in was being photographed. I told him that a photographer had to be on the scene of an event *before* it happened in order to photograph it. While reporters could put together news stories from interviews even if they hadn't witnessed an event personally, photographers could get photographs only at the time and on the scene.

Dr. King and the SCLC had kept their plans for nonviolent marches and demonstrations as secret as possible, so that neither the Klan nor local law enforcement authorities would disrupt the demonstration before it began. I suggested he phone me directly if he wanted me at a demonstration, and we exchanged home telephone numbers.

He began this direct relationship in very small ways, until he could trust me to keep dates and times of demonstrations in confidence. Our friendship was formed during that long evening in Miami. Outside of my immediate family, his was the greatest friendship I have ever known or experienced. The mutual trust grew and grew. A trust that I never abrogated. A trust that he showed in many ways in the ten years that followed.

Martin Luther King, Jr. — my friend.

Flip Schulke
July 1994

Dr. King, or "Doc" as his close friends and family called him, had this wonderful sense of humor. He was truly an optimist. He could always see the best side of any situation even when he saw and experienced the worst in others.

Because he was a Baptist minister, he had to be very serious in public. The times were serious. But after church with his congregation, his face would light up. I wish that more people could have seen this lighthearted side of him.

Prologue

This Is a Time of Shame and Sorrow
An Address by Robert F. Kennedy given the day after Martin Luther King, Jr.'s, assassination.

This is a time of shame and sorrow. . . . I have saved this one opportunity . . . to speak briefly to you about the mindless menace of violence in America which again stains our land and every one of our lives.

It is not the concern of any one race. The victims of violence are black and white, rich and poor, young and old, famous and unknown. They are, most important of all, human beings whom other human beings loved and needed. No one—no matter where he lives or what he does—can be certain who will suffer from some senseless act of bloodshed. And yet it goes on and on and on in this country of ours.

Why? What has violence ever accomplished? What has it ever created? No martyr's cause has ever been stilled by his assassin's bullet.

No wrongs have ever been righted by riots and civil disorders. A sniper is only a coward, not a hero, and an uncontrolled, uncontrollable mob is only the voice of madness, not the voice of reason.

Whenever any American's life is taken by another American unnecessarily—whether it is done in the name of the law or in the defiance of the law, by one man or a gang, in cold blood or in passion, in an attack of violence or in response to violence—whenever we tear at the fabric of the life which another man has painfully and clumsily woven for himself and his children, the whole nation is degraded.

"Among free men," said Abraham Lincoln. "there can be no successful appeal from the ballot to the bullet; and those who take such appeal are sure to lose their cause and pay the costs."

Yet we seemingly tolerate a rising level of violence that ignores our common humanity and our claims to civilization alike. We calmly accept newspaper reports of civilian slaughter in far-off lands. We glorify killing on movie and television screens and call it entertainment. We make it easy for men of all shades of sanity to acquire whatever weapons and ammunition they desire.

Too often we honor swagger and bluster and the wielders of force, too often we excuse those who are willing to build their own lives on the shattered dreams of others. Some Americans who preach nonviolence abroad fail to practice it here at home. Some who accuse others of inciting riots have by their own conduct invited them.

Some look for scapegoats, others look for conspiracies, but this much is clear: violence breeds violence, repression brings retaliation, and only a cleansing of our whole society can remove this sickness from our soul.

For there is another kind of violence, slower but just as deadly destructive as the shot or the bomb in the night. This is the violence of institutions; indifference and inaction and slow decay. This is the violence that afflicts the poor, that poisons relations between men because their skin has different colors. This is the slow destruction of a child by hunger, and schools without books and homes without heat in the winter.

This is the breaking of a man's spirit by denying him the chance to stand as a father and as a man among other men. And this too afflicts us all.

I have not come here to propose a set of specific remedies, nor is there a single set. For a broad and adequate outline we know what must be done. When you teach a man to hate and fear his brother, when you teach that he is a lesser man because of his color or his beliefs or the policies he pursues, when you teach that those who differ from you threaten your freedom or your job or your family, then you also learn to confront others not as fellow citizens but as enemies, to be met not with cooperation but with conquest; to be subjugated and mastered.

We learn, at the last, to look at our brothers as aliens, men with whom we share a city, but not a community, men bound to us in common dwelling, but not in common effort. We learn to share only a common fear, only a common desire to retreat from each other, only a common impulse to meet disagreement with force. For all this, there are no final answers.

Yet we know what we must do. It is to achieve true justice among our fellow citizens. The question is not what programs we should seek to enact. The question is whether we can find in our own midst and in our own hearts that leadership of humane purpose that will recognize the terrible truths of our existence.

We must admit the vanity of our false distinctions among men and learn to find our own

advancement in the search for the advancement of others. We must admit in ourselves that our own children's future cannot be built on the misfortunes of others. We must recognize that this short life can neither be ennobled nor enriched by hatred or revenge.

Our lives on this planet are too short and the work to be done too great to let this spirit flourish any longer in our land. Of course we cannot vanquish it with a program, nor with a resolution.

But we can perhaps remem-ber, if only for a time, that those who live with us are our brothers, that they share with us the same short moment of life; that they seek, as do we, nothing but the chance to live out their lives in purpose and in happiness, winning what satisfaction and fulfillment they can.

Surely this bond of common faith, this bond of common goal, can begin to teach us something. Surely we can learn, at least, to look at those around us as fellow men, and surely we can begin to work a little harder to bind up the wounds among us and to become in our own hearts brothers and countrymen once again.

—R.F.K., April 5, 1968

I was not in Memphis the day Dr. King was murdered on the balcony of the Lorraine Motel. I had not been able to interest *Life* or any other magazine in assigning me to cover the continuing protest marches of the Garbage Workers Union in Memphis. Instead, I was on a business trip in New York City, watching the six-o'clock news on television. I was more than shocked. Not only had a great American leader been assassinated, but a close personal friend.

Thoughts of Medgar Evers and John F. Kennedy flashed through my mind. Uppermost, though, were thoughts of Coretta and the King children. They had lived with this possibility for years. Could I be of any help? I phoned the picture desk at *Life* and offered my services. The editors declined, saying that they had already flown in a number of photographers to Atlanta. I then phoned Coretta. She asked where I was, and then asked me to fly to Atlanta and be with the family in the King home during the preparations for the funeral. "We need you to document this," she said.

I jumped on a plane and arrived at the King home late in the evening. Many journalists and photographers were stationed outside, and my friends among them told me that no one was being allowed inside. I rang the doorbell and was admitted instantly. With Coretta's permission, I phoned *Life* and was assigned for complete coverage.

Coretta was in their bedroom in the rear of the home. The children were asleep. Close family friends were taking care of the house, and the Reverend Ralph Abernathy was conferring about the funeral arrangements. Coretta and the Reverend Abernathy filled me in on what had happened in Memphis. Their trust made it possible for me to begin documenting what was happening. Jesse Jackson arrived, and he and other SCLC leaders spoke of their leader's death, sympathized with Coretta, and kept repeating, "What are we going to do? How do we replace Dr. King?" I knew the importance of photographing the grief that surrounded me, but it was one of the hardest things I have ever done.

Knowing that I could not photograph all of the events that the family experienced alone, I got Coretta's permission to telephone a young minister, Bob Fitch, who had worked with Dr. King and the SCLC in the past. He was a very good photographer who at the time was working with the United Farm Workers in California. He arrived and we split the necessary documentation between us. We played with the children and accompanied the family to the private and open viewings of Dr. King's body in a chapel of Spelman College. Mourners of all races, religions, and social classes came to pay their respects. Senator and Mrs. Robert F. Kennedy visited Coretta at the home. Who could have imagined that Senator Kennedy would also be assassinated two months later in Los Angeles?

The funeral service for Dr. King was held in Ebenezer Baptist Church. Coretta sat across the aisle from where Bob, Moneta Sleet of *Ebony* magazine, and I could photograph the service. The dignity of Coretta holding their youngest child, Bernice, was engraved in my mind. So too were the images of Martin Luther King, Sr., with his wife and the whole family in the front two church pews. Senator Hubert H. Humphrey, Mrs. John F. Kennedy, and many many more of the world's notables as well as hundreds of Dr. King's civil rights coworkers left powerful images.

I rode to the gravesite in Coretta's funeral car and thereby missed seeing the mule-drawn wagon that bore Dr. King's casket. Harry Belafonte sat beside Coretta at the gravesite. Their composure broke ever so slightly. I could see the terrible pain in their eyes through my camera lens—the hardest thing in the world is to focus through your own tears.

These photographs are a constant reminder of the violence that took three great men in their prime—Dr. Martin Luther King, Jr., John F. Kennedy, and Robert F. Kennedy.

Alberta Williams King and Reverend Martin Luther King, Sr.

Coretta Scott King with her children, Bernice, Martin III, and Dexter.

*Robert and Ethel
Kennedy pay their
respects with Coretta
Scott King at her home
in Atlanta, Georgia.*

*Vice President Hubert
H. Humphry at the
funeral service.*

*The King family in the
front two church pews
at the funeral.*

(Left) The empty pulpit of the Dexter Avenue Baptist Church, Dr. King's first pastorate, in Montgomery, Alabama.

(Right) Family friend, Harry Belafonte, with Coretta Scott King at the burial sight.

He had a Dream

Dexter Avenue Baptist Church, Montgomery, Alabama.

James Meredith applied to the University of Mississippi in the spring of 1961. His application was rejected. Thus began more than a year of legal struggle to force the university to admit Meredith to the undergraduate school. In September 1962, the U.S. Supreme Court upheld the lower-court decision to allow Meredith to attend.

Life sent me and a few others to Memphis, Tennessee, where we rented the largest car we could find—a four-door Cadillac. Why such a large car? Because at the time, it could outrun any segregationist's pickup truck, which was very important to life and limb when covering civil rights assignments in the deep South. We drove to Oxford, the home of the University of Mississippi. We could drive way over the speed limit. There were no highway patrol cars on the road the whole length of our trip, because they were all surrounding the university campus. More than one hundred patrol cars were blocking entrances to the campus.

On September 27, Meredith, accompanied by John Doar and Chief U.S. Marshal James J. P. McShane, was refused entrance to the campus by Lieutenant Governor Paul Johnson and scores of Mississippi highway officers and patrolmen *(left)*. On Sunday, September 30, a couple of government airplanes brought a few dozen U.S. marshals, many of whom were deputized from the Fish and Game Department. Meredith was nowhere to be seen. The marshals drove in army trucks to the front of the administration building. At this point, the highway patrol would no longer let the press onto the campus. Luckily, I had made a friend of a liberal university professor who lived on campus. He hid us in the trunk of his car and drove us, unseen, past the highway patrolmen guarding the entrance.

A large mob of students and segregationists were milling about the front of the administration building *(right)*. It was obvious that the highway patrol was letting the segregationists onto the campus and keeping everyone else off. On a pocket radio, I listened to President Kennedy give an address, in which he said: "Americans are free, in short, to disagree with the law, but not to disobey it. . . . No man, however prominent and powerful, and no mob, however unruly or boisterous, is entitled to defy a court of law." Near the end of the speech, tear gas was fired upon the mob by the marshals inside the administration building *(overleaf)*.

I was near the mob, feeling relatively safe, since I had hired a couple of university football players to watch my back. They thought it was great fun, and I wasn't worried about being blindsided. I took a few photographs of the mob and the tear gas before being overwhelmed *(continued on page 34)*

by the gas myself. I dove under some bushes and stayed there for a while, trying to get my eyesight back. After that experience, we all purchased gas masks for future civil rights assignments.

Stray rifle shots began to come from the buildings surrounding the campus square. I heard some footsteps on the sidewalk near me. Though it was dark, I could recognize the voice of Paul Guillard, a French journalist. I yelled at him to get down, that there had been shooting all around. He yelled back that "this is nothing compared to Cyprus." Since I had not been to the civil war in Cyprus, this experience was enough for me. I had good photographs, so I left the campus. Later that night, I learned that Paul Guillard had been slain by an unknown sniper.

President Kennedy federalized the Mississippi National Guard that night. The mob had attacked the administration building with a bulldozer and were barely held off by the marshals' use of tear gas from inside the building. Carloads of armed segregationists with Molotov cocktails continued to arrive, and sniper bullets were flying. Many marshals were wounded. Early Monday morning, additional military police and Oxford's unit of the Mississippi National Guard arrived. Ninety-three prisoners were taken, and the mob finally retreated.

Unbeknownst to the mob, Meredith had slept in a nearby dormitory through the night. He was registered at seven-thirty on Monday morning, after a sixteen-month legal battle. He graduated two years later. Martin Luther King said of him: "One day the South will recognize its real heroes. They will be the James Merediths, with the noble sense of purpose that enables them to face jeering and hostile mobs, and with the agonizing loneliness that characterizes the life of the pioneer."

The day after the rioting, James Meredith studied in his dormitory room (above).

*Reverend Martin
Luther King, Sr.,
introducing his son
to give the Sunday
sermon.*

Dr. King was an incredible and passionate speaker whose body movement reflected the emotion in his words. I wanted the sound of his voice and the words he spoke to be somehow visible in the silent, still photographs. His father, Daddy King, would not permit flash photography during church services in his Ebenezer Baptist Church. But Dr. King had prevailed upon him to let me photograph without flash during a Sunday service. In April 1964, I sat in the front pew, reserved for the church deacons, and photographed the whole service.

The hymns were infectious. I have no ear for singing, but joined in belting out the words. At one point in the service, Daddy King interrupted his sermon and said to the congregation, "We have a *Life* magazine photographer sitting in the front today who has joined in the service better than many of you." This surprised me. I was so impressed with the congregation's fellowship after the service that I returned another time to take additional photographs of Dr. King.

I also went to Ebenezer Church every time I was in Atlanta. Nearly every Sunday, Dr. King gave the sermon. He had the ability to use events in the local, national, and world news and relate them to the ethics and philosophy of his religion. His view of Christianity became entwined with his congregation's everyday life and work.

On August 28, 1963, the first large integrated protest march was held in Washington, D.C. The authorities and the media were convinced there would be riots. I, however, felt otherwise and did not want to be assigned to a military outfit on the outskirts of Washington, waiting for a riot that wouldn't happen. Northern media seemed to be more influenced by the rhetoric of the Black Muslim movement in Chicago and New York than by Martin Luther King and other nonviolent southern civil rights leaders. One northern editor told me that Martin Luther King, Jr., was a half-baked southern preacher interested in filling his own pockets and that his nonviolence was just a gimmick to make himself rich. "If any change comes," the editor said, "it will be led by the violent message of Malcolm X, not the religious preachings of King."

I disagreed with this commonly held view and accepted the job of directing a crew of photojournalists for a syndication of foreign magazines. I was responsible for covering the train station near the Capitol building and the area around the Washington Monument, which was the gathering place for the march. I photographed a

Many members of the civil rights group, CORE, wore the equality symbol on their foreheads.

45

multiracial group of marchers getting off the train; among them was a wonderful man waving a flag that said "FREEDOM" *(page 44).* I followed them. The leader asked me for the best route to the Washington Monument. I told him the shortest route was down Constitution Avenue but the most scenic route would be down the Mall between the Capitol and the Washington Monument. They took the scenic route. One of my favorite pictures is of the marchers with the Capitol dome behind them.

From the top of the Washington Monument, I took a picture of the thousands of marchers gathered around the Lincoln Memorial. I then walked through the Mall to join them and hear Dr. King speak. I knew he would give the best speech of the day. He was the last speaker of many, so the steps leading up to the podium on the Lincoln Memorial were not jammed; it was late afternoon and some of the listeners had grown tired and left. I found the photojournalist covering the speeches for our group. I told him it was his area, but I wanted to hear King speak. He said, "Great, I've had enough speakers. If you want to hear King speak, you photograph him and I can cut out." I told him that King would give the best speech and pictures of him would be the best of the day, *(continued on page 49)*

Marchers cheer after Dr. King's speech.

but my advice fell on deaf ears.

Dr. King took the podium and gave the "I Have a Dream" speech. I took dozens of pictures of Dr. King's speech, and to this day, I wish I had more. It was a defining moment in the nonviolent civil rights movement. Television and newspapers ran the pictures, the voice, and the words worldwide. Then, as now, the general public can only remember that great day as the "I Have a Dream" day. No other speakers are remembered. There was no violence that day, shocking the doomsayers. It was a day of peace and of the peacemaker—Martin Luther King, Jr.

"Free at last. Free at last. Thank God almighty, we are free at last." Dr. King ends his famous speech on the steps of the Lincoln Memorial.

54

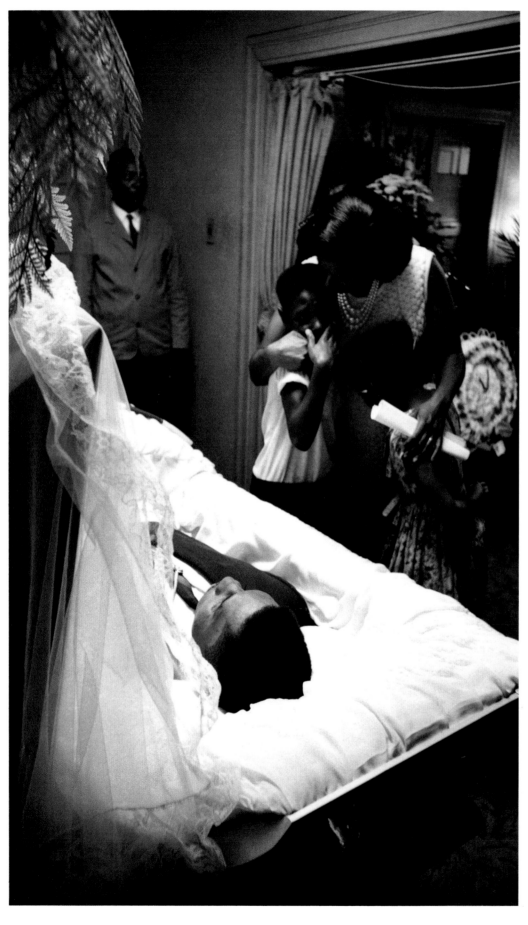

I was sent to Tuscaloosa, Alabama, on June 11, 1963, to photograph Governor George C. Wallace's attempt to stop the court-ordered integration of the University of Alabama by "standing in the schoolhouse door." Only after President John F. Kennedy federalized the Alabama National Guard did Governor Wallace cease blocking the entrance of the Negro students.

I was awakened in the middle of the night by a phone call telling me to drive to Jackson, Mississippi. A top leader of the National Association for the Advancement of Colored People (NAACP) had been shot and killed in front of his home after midnight. Driving as quickly as we could, a *Life* reporter and I arrived at the home of Medgar Evers. Twenty or twenty-five reporters and photographers were camped in their cars and on the sidewalk in front of the house. I could see the bullet holes in the front windowpanes *(page 58)*.

As I walked up to the front door, a couple of my journalist friends told me that Mrs. Evers was not letting any of the press into the house. It never hurts to try, so I knocked on the door. Myrlie Evers came to the door. What I said to her and what she said to me I cannot remember. She asked me in, and I began to document the scenes of the distraught family and their grieving friends. No one seemed to notice me at all. In fact, everyone was worried about whether or not I had had something to eat. It seemed to me that I was accepted as part of the mourning group surrounding the Evers family. It turned out that I was the only press person given access to the family.

Two days later, Myrlie and her children, Darrell and Rena, went to the funeral home to view Medgar's body before the public viewing. Someone said to jump into Charles Evers's car—he was Medgar's brother. He took me into the small viewing room, where the casket was open. Suddenly, I noticed that the only people in the room were Myrlie, the children, and Charles *(left)*. I stood in a corner of the room behind the casket as Mrs. Evers and the children stood looking at the dead husband and father.

I thought of the privacy I was invading with my camera. But the words of Dr. King went through my mind: "The pain and torture that we as a people are going through must be shown as clearly as possible to the American people." Those words kept me there, but did not keep me from being overwhelmed emotionally. Was it right to do this as a photo-journalist?

Four years later in 1967, Myrlie Evers published her book *For Us, the Living*, in which I found the following account:

A *Life* photographer appeared from nowhere and was there constantly, in the house, outside, and he followed me when I took Darrell and Rena to the funeral home. I hated it and didn't know who had given him

permission, but I could never remember to ask anyone.

Medgar had been dressed in the clothes that I had selected for him. I asked the funeral director to have the others leave so the children and I could be alone. Everyone left but the *Life* photographer, who went on snapping pictures. I had thought about bringing the children to see their father dead, and I had thought and thought. My natural impulse was not to do it, but I remembered the way they had last seen him, his broken body stretched out in a pool of blood, the terror and ugliness and hatred of that night, and I decided that Darrell and Rena should see him once again, peaceful and at rest.

I had said I wanted the casket closed at the funeral, and this was the last opportunity, so I brought them with me, and he did look peaceful, and I think it helped. The children left after a moment. I stayed. The tired lines were gone from his face, and I had a terrible urge to hold his head and stroke his temples and say that everything would be all right. And then I sensed that I was not alone. I turned and the *Life* photographer was there. His eyes were filled with tears. For the first time since Medgar's death the hatred I had felt for all whites was gone. It never returned.*

Upon hearing of Medgar Evers's death, Dr. King said: "This tragic occurrence should cause all persons of good will to be aroused and...to be more determined than ever before to break down

*Myrlie Evers with William Peters, *For Us, the Living* (Doubleday, 1967), pp. 314–15.

all of the barriers of racial segregation and discrimination, and I'm sure that the movement in the South will go on and that the movement in Mississippi will go on—even in a more determined manner as a result of this dastardly act on the part of those who are against democracy." Almost four thousand people, including civil rights workers and leaders from all over the country, came to the Masonic temple in Jackson, which doubled as the state headquarters for

the NAACP. Dr. King attended, along with the Reverend Ralph Abernathy and many other SCLC field workers *(above)*.

Medgar's brother, Charles, told me that the body would be taken from Jackson by train to Washington, D.C., the day after the memorial service. Medgar would be buried in Arlington Cemetery. Charles suggested I accompany the family on the train trip, and of course I accepted. This was the first murder of a black civil rights

leader the media had paid any attention to. I felt that the nation as a whole had little knowledge of the abuses of the segregation system in the South.

At any funeral service, emotions flow over you. The songs and hymns and the obvious suffering of the family affect all of those involved. I wanted to show the grief that Mrs. Evers was going through, so I positioned myself to be able to show her face from the side. During the service, one tear ran down her cheek *(page 59)*. The

*Medgar Evers'
daughter, Rena, at
her father's funeral.*

picture summed up both her suffering and all the suffering of southern black families at that time. With Mrs. Evers's permission, I gave the photograph to the NAACP, which used it as a poster for many years. After the service a nonviolent memorial march was held, going from the Masonic temple to downtown Jackson. As the march reached downtown, the police tried to stop it and bloodied the heads of many demonstrators.

An ardent segregationist, Byron de la Beckwith, was later charged with the murder of Medgar Evers, but after two trials, each resulting in a hung jury, de la Beckwith went unpunished. In 1994, thirty-one years later, Byron de la Beckwith was indicted by the State of Mississippi for a third time. Because of a massive change in both the legal system and the citizens of Mississippi, de la Beckwith was finally found guilty of the murder of Medgar Evers.

I accompanied the Evers family to Washington, D.C., and to his burial at Arlington National Cemetery. Little did I imagine when I heard the honor guard's rifle volley that I would return to the sound of cannons later that year for the burial of President John F. Kennedy, and again in 1968 for the burial of Robert F. Kennedy. All were felled by assassins' bullets.

In September 1963, the federal court had ordered Governor George Wallace to integrate specific schools in Mobile, Montgomery, and Huntsville, Alabama. *Life* sent a reporter with me to Montgomery, the state capital, to document Governor Wallace during the crisis.

Wallace had agreed that the *Life* reporter and I could spend some time in his office, documenting the unfolding events. He and his staff held a very stiff and formal meeting. At the end of the meeting, all of the reporters present were ushered out of his office. I was allowed to stay in order to take candid photographs *(right)*.

As soon as the reporters left, the subject changed to methods the highway patrol should use to keep the "niggers" out of the schools. How to get around the court orders was next on the agenda, followed by a discussion of payoffs for road contractors. It seemed as if I wasn't even in the room. All I could conclude at the time was that Wallace and his staff had a very limited under-standing of my profession and thought I was either deaf or disin-terested in what was being said.

Every so often I would excuse myself to make a trip to the rest room, where the *Life* reporter waited for me. I would quickly tell the reporter all that I had heard and then return to the governor's office. Needless to say, after some of the conversations began to ap-pear in print, I was never allowed inside the governor's office again.

Wallace and his staff became very wary of photographers.

After that day with Governor Wallace, I took such a personal dislike to him as an individual that I realized I could not be fair to him in any future public event, and I turned down subsequent assignments on his activities.

The Alabama highway patrolmen were stationed in front of the Montgomery High School. It was the day appointed for the integration of Alabama's schools. I noticed that one patrolman had his child's photograph mounted under the clear plastic grip of his pistol. I could never understand how a person could place the likeness of a loved one on a weapon he might use to injure or kill someone. In my mind, it became a symbol of the segregationist mentality.

Colonel Al Lingo (dark glasses), Alabama Highway Department of Public Safety Director, outside the Montgomery High School.

The Supreme Court's order to desegregate the public schools was met with anger, hatred, and resistance. Montgomery, Alabama.

All of the students of the Montgomery
High School exited the school as the
first couple of Negro students were
escorted inside by the federal authorities.
The white students began to yell and
chant epithets at the top of their lungs.
A typical blond southern belle stood in
line and yelled words that I had not
heard used in public at that time. The
southern belle was supposed to be,
above all, a lady. Her yelling distorted
her face and showed her hatred. I
have always wondered if her beliefs
changed as she grew older.

Inside the office of one of Alabama's leading segregationist organizations.

*Joining the white
student protest
outside the
Montgomery High
School were
various hate groups—
Ku Klux Klan and
White Citizens'
Council members—
all carrying signs
reflecting their beliefs.*

Dr. King giving the Sunday sermon in the Ebeneezer Baptist Church in Atlanta, Georgia.

Dr. King greets churchgoers outside Ebeneezer Baptist Church.

Coretta, Yolanda (Yoki), Bernice (Bunny), and a parishiner.

*Dr. King with
Martin III (Marty).*

Occasionally, after I had heard Dr. King speak in Ebenezer Church, he would invite me to his house for Sunday lunch. I shared his love for southern fried chicken, and Coretta always had the best at the King home.

I'll always remember the Sunday I took photographs of King at home with Coretta and the children—Yoki, Marty, Dexter, and Bunny. On previous occasions, I had respected his wishes for "photographic privacy" and left my cameras outside. It was good to relax and let the conversation go where it would, sometimes away from the problems of the civil rights struggle and its ever present danger.

When I got out of the car on this particular Sunday, King turned to me and said, "Why don't you bring in your cameras?" I was obviously puzzled, and he said, "It isn't every day one learns that one has won the Nobel Peace Prize!"

I stuttered a quick "Congratulations" and photographed King and Marty walking up the steps to the front door. Inside, while I took more photographs, I asked him when and where the Nobel ceremony would be held. "December 10, in Oslo, Norway," *(continued on page 78)*

Dr. King plays ball with daughter Yoki.

*Coretta and
daughter Bunny.*

he told me. On hearing that, I made up my mind to get *Life* or some other magazine to send me there to document his great achievement.

We had lunch in the dining room, where a portrait of Gandhi hung overlooking the table *(page 79)*. Phone calls came in all the time. King received congratulations for the Peace Prize from all over the nation. A foreign TV crew from Norway knocked at the door, and King let them take some film of the family eating Sunday dinner. When the TV crew left, the kids went to play in the backyard, followed by their father. King spent special time with each child, and it was easy to see just how close they were to their father. I had been around the house so often that no one paid any attention to me darting about catching the family at play.

On other occasions at the house, I had observed the hugging and hand-holding between King and Coretta. They had been through a lot together, and their love, trust, and respect for each other were apparent. I often told Dr. King just how lucky he was to come home to Atlanta nearly every week because his father wanted him to give the Sunday sermon. He knew that I too had four children, and they too worried

Dr. King and son Dexter.

about their father, since all they saw of the civil rights movement was the violent demonstrations on TV. I rarely got home to be with my wife and children on weekends.

That day ended with hundreds of family photos in my camera bag. After seeing the developed photographs, I knew I had captured Martin Luther King, Jr., family man, exactly as I knew him to be. Only a couple of my photographs of King as a loving family man were published in American magazines during his lifetime. J. Edgar Hoover and the FBI had a field day trying to defame the character and reputation of King. I think my photographs taken on that November in 1964 put to rest Hoover's character assassination attempts.

I did not get to Oslo, Norway, for the Nobel Peace Prize ceremony. It is hard to believe now, but no magazine, including *Life*, was interested in covering it. They all said, "We'll get the pix off the wires." The fact is, no American publication—newspaper or magazine sent a photojournalism team to the ceremonies, except for *Ebony*. Only John Johnson, the editor and owner of *Ebony*, understood the importance of that Peace Prize event.

(Left) Coretta with Bunny, Marty, and Yoki.

(Right) Dr. King with son Marty.

(Left) Dexter with his father.

(Right) Daughter Bunny being tossed into the air.

Bunny and her father.

*(Left) Yoki with her
father.*

Dr. King and his son Dexter.

*Because his office
was so small, Dr. King
often met with his
SCLC staff in a res-
taurant on Atlanta's
Auburn Street.*

Marchers cross the Edmund Pettus Bridge in Selma, Alabama, and are stopped by the Alabama Highway Patrol.

Beginning in 1965, the Student Nonviolent Coordinating Committee (SNCC) and the SCLC concentrated on voter registration in the town of Selma, Alabama. On March 7, a group of protest marchers led by SNCC's John Lewis and SCLC's Hosea Williams were beaten when attempting to cross the Edmund Pettus Bridge on the road to Montgomery. They were gassed and clubbed by state highway patrolmen under the direction of Al Lingo, as well as sheriff's deputies under the leadership of Jim Clark. An order by Governor Wallace had prohibited the one-hundred-mile march from Selma to Montgomery.

Newspaper and television cameramen caught the beatings, and the images were seen on the news that evening across the nation. Dr. King was not in Selma that day; he was in Atlanta giving the Sunday sermon at Ebenezer Baptist Church. I was in Miami for a weekend with my family. I had been in Selma, but it had appeared quiet, so I had gone home for a few days off.

I saw the teargassing and beatings on Miami television and phoned Dr. King in Atlanta. He asked me to fly to Atlanta and then accompany him to Montgomery, where we were to attend a meeting that evening of all the top civil rights leaders in order to plan responses to the Selma events. So I met him in Atlanta, flew with him to Montgomery, and went with him to a little house in Montgomery's Negro district. All of the most prominent leaders of SCLC, NAACP, CORE (Congress for Racial Equality), SNCC, and the Urban League were crowded inside the tiny living room. I was the only white man there. James Farmer, the head of CORE, quickly spoke up. "What's a white man doing here? I'm not going to say anything while a white man is here." Martin responded: "Look, I have known this man for years. Not only is he a friend of mine, I have his assurance that nothing will go beyond this room that isn't cleared. He just wants to photograph us debating." Farmer kept complaining, and King spoke again: "What are we doing here? We are trying to fight for integration." King responded with a statement I will never forget: "I don't care if Flip is purple with yellow polka dots, he is a human being and I know him better than I know a lot of black people. I trust him. He stays and that's it."

So I stayed and photographed and had no further acceptance problems. Later, King and I discussed the evening's tensions. I saw that he was living what he preached. He said that if you kept people out, you were no better than the system he was trying to change. He believed in mankind as a whole and that we were all children of God. He was very much opposed to separatism of any kind. He really did not see my color, and he proved it that evening in that little house on the

outskirts of Montgomery.

Dr. King went to Selma the next day and spoke to the protest marchers who were gathered awaiting the chance to march from Selma to Montgomery. A police line had been set up on the outskirts of the Selma Negro district. There were Alabama highway patrolmen, Selma policemen, sheriff's deputies, and the sheriff's posse made up of local segregationists.

No marcher could cross the police line. Governor Wallace would not permit the march from Selma to Montgomery. From all over the United States, thousands of people, black and white, came to Selma to join the protest. As the numbers increased, the atmosphere grew more tense. White protesters were turned away from white churches on Sunday. James Reeb, a white Unitarian minister who was in Selma to join the protest, was beaten by four segregationists and died two days later. Catholic nuns and priests came to Selma, even though the area's presiding bishop forbade them to come to his diocese.

The marchers manned the police line day and night, rain or shine, and tempers flared. At one point, there was a shoving match near the line, and some children around eight to ten years old were among the protesters who were shoved to the ground. I stopped taking pictures. I had children of my own, the same age, so I jumped into the fray and tried, along

with the other protesters, to push the segregationists off.

That evening, after the protest rally, Dr. King came up to me and said, "Oh, I hear you're becoming violent. You're supposed to practice nonviolence also." I asked him what he was talking about. He said, "You jumped in today when some children were being shoved to the ground. That's not your job. Your job is to photograph what is happening to us." He asked me if the children were being badly hurt, and I said no. He then said: "Listen, you were the only photographer at that incident. We as a people have been beaten and murdered for a couple hundred years. What is important is for you to do what you are supposed to do, and that is to record and communicate to the rest of the world what is going on here. You have to stay back, and not listen to your guts. You've got to do what you were sent here to do, and that is to keep the camera shooting."

Considering all that King was involved in at Selma, I was surprised that he would spend the time to sit down and explain to me how to be a better photojournalist. He had a way of bawling you out, and you felt good at the end of it. He had the most wonderful way of doing that. He'd give you a hug and you would die for the man.

*The police line on the
outskirts of Selma's
Negro district.*

*Dr. King speaking
to the protesters
waiting to march
from Selma to
Montgomery.*

Marchers wait behind police barricades.

*Dr. King with other
civil rights leaders in
Montgomery. Reverend
Andrew Young (far left)
and Reverend Hosea
Williams (sitting).*

Catholic nuns and priests protesting in Selma, even though the presiding bishop forbade them to come to his diocese.

*Participants in a rally
held in Brown's
Chapel in Selma.*

Selma protest marchers
manning the police line
rain or shine.

Dallas County Sheriff, James G. Clark (dark glasses), lead a group of deputies on horseback involved in the first beatings of marchers on the Edmund Pettus Bridge.

Dr. King and Reverend Ralph Abernathy, vice president of SCLC and King's best personal friend, at one of the rallies in Selma.

A memorial service for Unitarian minister James Reeb, beaten to death by segregationists in Selma, is held on March 12, 1965, outside the Selma City Hall. The service was led by Archbishop Iakovos of the Greek Orthodox Church, Walter Reuther president of the UAW, Dr. King, and civil rights leader Reverend Fred Shuttlesworth.

*Primary election day,
April 1966, in Greene
County, Alabama.*

In April of 1966, the first primary elections were held in Alabama in which Negroes were able to vote in any numbers since Reconstruction following the Civil War. I had covered the voter registration campaigns in Greene and Wilcox counties during the summer of 1964 and wanted to document the actual day of voting.

Outside a polling place in a small Alabama town, I noticed a number of beat-up pickup trucks parked close to the entrance of the voting precinct. Walking past the empty trucks, I saw rifles tucked into rifle racks in the back windows *(left)*. No one was in sight on the street and sidewalk in this area except for the long line of waiting voters, all of whom were black.

Thinking that perhaps this obvious display of firepower was a silent warning to blacks who wanted to vote, I stuck my head inside an open truck window. I took a couple of photographs and was suddenly grabbed from behind by an angry-looking white man in overalls. He accused me of violating his private property. A crowd of angry whites soon gathered, coming out of a nearby bar that I had failed to notice earlier. Threats spewed forth. I figured that I had gotten myself into a real mess. Two years before, the three civil rights workers James Chaney, Andrew Goodman, and Michael Schwerner had been murdered

(continued on page 119)

117

A long line of black voters awaiting their turn at the ballot.

and buried near the town of Philadelphia, Mississippi.

As the group started discussing among themselves just where, out of town, they would take me and the *Life* reporter with me, two uniformed policemen walked up. They told the segregationists to let us go. Of course, they argued with the policemen, whom they all knew. It was a very small town. I'll never forget what one of the policemen said: "I'd like to take them out to the woods with you, and let you all do what you want to them. But George [Governor Wallace] told all of us that he doesn't want one single problem on voting day, because the New York Jew nigger press will feature it on the front page. So you've got to let them go."

He took us over to his police car and said: "I hate you commies just as much as those boys over there, but can't do anything about it today. Get into your car and drive right out of town. I'll be right behind, to 'protect' you." His voice was dripping with redneck sarcasm.

We got out. I had the photograph I wanted. Driving away, I thought to myself, "Now I owe my life, or at least the escape from a good beating, to Governor George Wallace. What an unlikely rescuer."

Thomas E. Gilmore campaigns for sheriff of Greene County, Alabama, in April 1966. He lost his first election but was subsequently elected sheriff at the next election.

*Thomas E. Gilmore
(right) speaking with
a potential voter.*

*James Meredith's
"March Against Fear"
through Mississippi in
June 1966.*

In June of 1966, James Meredith, the first black undergraduate of the University of Mississippi, lead the "March Against Fear" to further black voter registration and voting rights. He was shot from ambush at the very beginning of his march. Hospitalized for gun wounds, Meredith called upon the civil rights organizations and people across the nation to come to Mississippi and carry on his march. At first hundreds, and then thousands joined the trek down the length of the state.

Dr. King joined the march at different points, and led a side march, diverging from the main route into the city of Philadelphia, Mississippi, and through Neshoba County, where the three civil rights workers—James Chaney, Andrew Goodman, and Michael Schwerner—had been murdered in 1964. The marchers went from the black section of Philadelphia, under the watch of the Mississippi State Troopers, to the Neshoba County Court House in the town's square.

Dr. King, Reverend Abernathy, Andrew Young, and the other march leaders stood on the courthouse steps and held a short memorial service for the slain civil rights workers. Speaking through a handheld megaphone, Dr. King said that the killers of the three civil rights workers were probably within earshot of his voice. From a second-floor courthouse window, a voice

(continued on page 127)

shouted out, "We're right behind you." Both Neshoba County sheriff Rainey and his deputy, Cecil Price, could be seen in the window. Though charged with complicity in the deaths, neither had been brought to trial at that time.

Years later, Reverend Abernathy told me in an interview how he felt that day: "Standing on those Neshoba Court House steps was the most frightening experience of my whole life. Dr. King always liked me to give the invocation and benediction prayers during any civil rights march. I gave the prayer at the end of the service, and I have always shut my eyes when I pray to God. But on those courthouse steps, surrounded by all that hate, I kept my eyes open all during my prayer. I never thought we would leave there alive."

Dr. King speaking at the state capitol in Jackson, Mississippi.

On the steps of the Neshoba County Court House, Philadelphia, Mississippi. Dr. King later remarked: "That day in Philadelphia, when I was speaking and Sheriff Rainey was behind me . . . I started saying the murderers were probably around, and some man behind me said, 'You're damn right. We're right behind you.' . . . I just knew I'd never see the end of that day."

It was during the "March Against Fear" that the slogan "Black Power" was first used in public speeches before reporters. SNCC's president, Stokely Carmichael, and his assistant, Willie Ricks, used the term; and soon after Black Panther signs appeared, and remained for the rest of the march. This was also an indication of the generational gap between the SCLC and SNCC. At times Dr. King despaired at trying to keep the southern civil rights movement on a nonviolent path. He said: "Violence as a way of achieving racial justice is both impractical and immoral. It is impractical because it is a descending spiral ending in destruction for all. The old law of an eye for an eye leaves everyone blind. It is immoral because it seeks to humiliate the opponent rather than win his understanding; it seeks to annihilate rather than convert. Violence is immoral because it thrives on hatred rather than love. It destroys community and makes brotherhood impossible. It leaves society in monologue rather than dialogue. Violence ends by defeating itself. It creates bitterness in the survivors and brutality in the destroyers."

After being teargassed by Mississippi state troopers in the towns of both Greenville and Canton, Dr. King said in a march rally speech: "I will never sink so low as to use violence or become violent."

Protesters giving the Black Power symbol and support for the Black Panther party.

Dr. King speaking to crowds about the importance of voting.

On October 30, 1967, the United States Supreme Court upheld lower court convictions of Dr. King and other members of the SCLC for trespass violations during the 1963 protest marches in Birmingham, Alabama. Dr. King and his aides had to fly from Atlanta to Montgomery to serve the four-day jail sentence.

I met him walking through the Atlanta airport. He was casually dressed in a sweater with the Bible and two other books under his arm. We boarded the flight to Montgomery together and he motioned for me to sit with him. At first he was deep in thought, but after a few moments he turned to me and asked about my wife and children in Miami. We exchanged some small talk and I asked him why he was moving about in public, through airports, and at conferences, with so much advance notice. I told him that I was worried about all the loose talk I had heard through the South about the need to "get rid of Martin Luther King."

He picked up the Bible from his lap and said: "I will be here as long as God wants me here. I am not being careless with my life, I'm not going to walk in front of a car. But I also don't fear death. When the Lord wants to take me, he will." I admitted to Dr. King that I did not have such faith. He spent quite a few minutes more counseling me

(continued on page 145)

about how I could develop and increase my faith. What had started out as my trying to tell him to be more careful, ended up with him worrying about my personal faith. He was going to jail and had been facing increasing problems with violent black protests, and he was more concerned about me than his own troubles.

I often find myself remembering that conversation, and it has been a great source of strength in my life. It was also the last personal conversation I had with Dr. King, and the last time I saw him alive.

Appendix

A Photograph of Mrs. Martin Luther King on the Cover of *Life*

I.
Your head—carved stone through which the hurt blood flows.
Three hundred years of anguish made this face
where now there glows
unbearable grace-in-grief and grief-in-grace.

Your body does not bend. It is one long cry.
Your mouth is silent, having too much to say.
The photo shows, deep as time, your left eye.
Our white bones sing the blues on this black day.

Keep, keep your harsh control. We fear
that if you wept, we also would lose all,
as if not only a tear,
but the hovering sky would fall.

II.
Your unbitter face bruises our eyes.
Beyond the blaze of bestiality
which brought you here—the fury of flowers.
Only your hands weep. Fighting his grief, we see
in front of you, suddenly, a tall man cries.
We suffer the live wound of these hours.

A wasp's bite, without fire, burns.
Today, a tree branch rattles the wind's teeth.
We vomit the word, "progress," when the country yearns
back toward the caveman's hide and the brute beneath.

You dignify this too degraded day.
We do not deserve your face with its assurance
that you bless us in this moment when we may
endure the terrible power of your endurance.

III.
The black, transparent veil protects
the brown veil of your face, and that protects
the red veil of your heart, and that protects
these people and this country as nothing else protects.

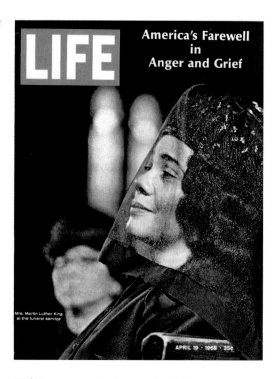

LIFE — America's Farewell in Anger and Grief

Mrs. Martin Luther King at the funeral service

APRIL 19 · 1968 · 35¢

"This poem belongs to Flip Schulke, for without his photograph, I would not have written it."
—Paul Engle, May 11, 1968

"You can kill a man but you can't kill an idea"

Mrs. Medgar W. Evers, widow of slain NAACP Mississippi State Field Secretary

KEEP THE IDEA OF FREEDOM ALIVE

JOIN NAACP

Chronology

1929	**1929** **January 15.** Martin Luther King, Jr., is born to the Reverend Martin Luther King and his wife, née Alberta Christine Williams, in Atlanta, Georgia.
1935–1944	**1935–1944** King attends David T. Howard Elementary School, Atlanta University Laboratory School, and Booker T. Washington High School. He passes the entrance examination to Morehouse College (Atlanta) before graduating from high school.
1947	**1947** King is licensed to preach and becomes assistant to his father, who is pastor of the Ebenezer Baptist Church in Atlanta.
1948	**1948** **February 25.** King is ordained to the Baptist ministry. **June.** King graduates from Morehouse College with a B.A. degree in sociology. **September.** King enters Crozer Theological Seminary in Chester, Pennsylvania. After hearing Dr. A. J. Muste and Dr. Mordecai W. Johnson preach on the life and teachings of Mahatma Gandhi, he begins to study Gandhi seriously.
1951	**1951** **June.** King graduates from Crozer with a B.D. degree.
1953	**1953** **June 18.** King marries Coretta Scott in Marion, Alabama.
1954	**1954** **May 17.** The Supreme Court rules unanimously in *Brown v. Board of Education* that racial segregation in public schools is unconstitutional. **October 31.** King is installed by the Reverend Martin Luther King, Sr., as the twentieth pastor of the Dexter Avenue Church in Montgomery.
1955	**1955** **June 5.** King receives a Ph.D. degree in systematic theology from Boston University. **November 17.** The Kings' first child, Yolanda Denise, is born in Montgomery. **December 1.** Mrs. Rosa Parks, a forty-two-year-old Montgomery seamstress, refuses to relinquish her bus seat to a white man, and is arrested.

1955 *(continued)*

December 5. The first day of the bus boycott. The trial of Rosa Parks. A meeting of movement leaders is held. Dr. King is unanimously elected president of an organization named the Montgomery Improvement Association, a name proposed by the Reverend Ralph Abernathy.

December 10. The Montgomery Bus Company suspends service in black neighborhoods.

1956

1956

January 26. Dr. King is arrested on a charge of traveling thirty miles an hour in a twenty-five-mile-an-hour zone in Montgomery. He is released on his own recognizance.

January 30. A bomb is thrown onto the porch of Dr. King's Montgomery home. Mrs. King and Mrs. Roscoe Williams, wife of a church member, are in the house with baby Yolanda Denise; no one is injured.

February 2. A suit is filed in federal district court asking that Montgomery's travel segregation laws be declared unconstitutional.

February 21. Dr. King is indicted with other figures in the Montgomery bus boycott on the charge of being party to a conspiracy to hinder and prevent the operation of business without "just or legal cause."

June 4. The federal district court rules that racial segregation on city bus lines is unconstitutional.

June 27. Dr. King is the guest speaker at the annual NAACP convention in San Francisco.

August 10. Dr. King is a speaker before the platform committee of the Democratic Party in Chicago.

October 30. Mayor Gyle of Montgomery instructs the city's legal department "to file such proceedings as it may deem proper to stop the operation of car pools and transportation systems growing out of the boycott."

November 13. The Supreme Court affirms the decision of the three-judge district court in declaring Alabama's state and local laws requiring segregation on buses unconstitutional.

December 20. Federal injunctions prohibiting segregation on buses are served on city and bus company officials in Montgomery. Injunctions are also served on state officials.

December 21. Montgomery buses are integrated.

1957

1957

January 10–11. The Southern Christian Leadership Conference (SCLC) is formed at the Ebenezer Baptist Church. Dr. King is elected its president.

January 27. An unexploded bomb is discovered on Dr. and Mrs. King's front porch.

1957 *(continued)*

February 18. *Time* magazine puts Dr. King on its cover.

May 17. Dr. King delivers a speech for the Prayer Pilgrimage for Freedom celebrating the third anniversary of the Supreme Court's desegregation decision. The speech, entitled "Give Us the Ballot," is given at the Lincoln Memorial in Washington, D.C.

June 13. Dr. King has a conference with Vice President Richard M. Nixon.

September. President Dwight D. Eisenhower federalizes the Arkansas National Guard to escort nine Negro students to an all-white high school in Little Rock, Arkansas.

September 2. Dr. King addresses a Labor Day seminar on the twenty-fifth anniversary of the Highlander Folk School, Monteagle, Tennessee.

September 9. The first civil rights act since Reconstruction is passed by Congress, creating the Civil Rights Commission and the Civil Rights Division of the Department of Justice.

October 23. A second child, Martin Luther III, is born to Dr. and Mrs. King.

1958

1958

February 8. Dr. King is a guest speaker at a legislative conference of the American Jewish Congress in New York.

June 23. Dr. King, along with Roy Wilkins of the NAACP, A. Philip Randolph, and Lester Granger, meets with President Dwight D. Eisenhower.

September 3. Dr. King is arrested on a charge of loitering (later changed to "failure to obey an officer") in the vicinity of the Montgomery recorder's court. He is released on $100 bond.

September 4. Dr. King is convicted after pleading not guilty on the charge of failure to obey an officer. Montgomery police commissioner Clyde C. Sellers, in an attempt to avoid the barrage of national press covering Dr. King's arrest, paid the fine almost immediately.

September 17. Dr. King's book *Stride Toward Freedom: The Montgomery Story* is published by Harper & Row.

September 20. Dr. King is stabbed in the chest by Izola Curry, forty-two; Mrs. Curry is subsequently alleged to be mentally deranged. The stabbing occurs in the heart of Harlem while Dr. King is autographing his recently published book. His condition is said to be serious but not critical.

1959

1959

January 30. Dr. King meets with Walter Reuther, president of the United Auto Workers union, in Detroit.

February 2–March 10. Dr. and Mrs. King spend a month in India studying Gandhi's techniques of nonviolence, as

1959 *(continued)*

guests of Prime Minister Nehru.

August 20. Dr. King delivers a speech to the National Bar Association in Milwaukee, Wisconsin.

November 29. Dr. King submits his resignation, effective on the fourth Sunday of January 1960, as pastor of the Dexter Avenue Baptist Church.

1960

1960

January 24. The King family moves to Atlanta. Dr. King becomes copastor, with his father, of Ebenezer Baptist Church.

February 1. The first lunch-counter sit-in to desegregate eating facilities is held by students in Greensboro, North Carolina.

February 17. A warrant is issued for Dr. King's arrest on charges that he did not pay his 1956 and 1958 Alabama state income taxes.

April 15. The Student Nonviolent Coordinating Committee (SNCC) is founded to coordinate student protest at Shaw University, Raleigh, North Carolina, on a temporary basis. (It is to become a permanent organization in October 1960.) Dr. King and James Lawson are the keynote speakers at the Shaw University founding.

May 28. Dr. King is acquitted of the tax evasion charge by an all-white jury in Montgomery.

June 10. Dr. King and A. Philip Randolph announce plans for picketing both the Republican and Democratic national conventions.

June 24. Dr. King has a conference with presidential candidate John F. Kennedy about racial matters.

October 19. Dr. King is arrested at an Atlanta sit-in and is jailed on a charge of violating the state's trespass law.

October 22–27. The Atlanta charges are dropped. All jailed demonstrators are released except for Dr. King, who is ordered held on a charge of violating a probated sentence in a traffic arrest case. He is transferred to the DeKalb County Jail in Decatur, Georgia, and is then transferred to the Reidsville State Prison on a $2000 bond. After a conversation between the presiding judge and John F. Kennedy's presidential campaign manager, Robert F. Kennedy, Dr. King is released on bail.

1961

1961

January 30. A third child, Dexter Scott, is born to Dr. and Mrs. King in Atlanta.

May 4. The first group of Freedom Riders, intent on integrating interstate buses, leaves Washington, D.C., by Greyhound bus. The group, organized by the Congress for Racial Equality (CORE), leaves shortly after the Supreme Court has outlawed

1961 *(continued)*

segregation in interstate transportation terminals. The bus is burned by segregationists outside of Anniston, Alabama, on May 14. A mob beats the Riders upon their arrival in Birmingham. The Riders are arrested in Jackson, Mississippi, and spend forty to sixty days in Parchman Penitentiary.

December 15. Dr. King arrives in Albany, Georgia, in response to a call from Dr. W. G. Anderson, the leader of the Albany movement to desegregate public facilities, which began in January 1961.

December 16. Dr. King is arrested at an Albany demonstration. He is charged with obstructing the sidewalk and parading without a permit.

1962

1962

February 27. Dr. King is tried and convicted for leading the December march in Albany.

May 2. Dr. King is invited to join the Birmingham protests.

July 27. Dr. King is arrested at an Albany city hall prayer vigil and jailed on charges of failure to obey a police officer, obstructing the sidewalk, and disorderly conduct.

September 20. James Meredith makes his first attempt to enroll at the University of Mississippi. He is actually enrolled by Supreme Court order and is escorted onto the Oxford, Mississippi, campus by U.S. marshals on October 1, 1962.

October 16. Dr. King meets with President John F. Kennedy at the White House for a one-hour conference.

1963

1963

March 28. The Kings' fourth child, Bernice Albertine, is born.

March–April. Sit-in demonstrations are held in Birmingham to protest segregation of eating facilities. Dr. King is arrested during a demonstration.

April 16. Dr. King writes the "Letter from Birmingham Jail" while imprisoned for demonstrating.

May 3–5. Eugene "Bull" Connor, director of public safety of Birmingham, orders the use of police dogs and fire hoses upon the marching protesters (young adults and children).

May 20. The Supreme Court of the United States rules Birmingham's segregation ordinances unconstitutional.

June 11. Governor George C. Wallace tries to stop the court-ordered integration of the University of Alabama by "standing in the schoolhouse door" and personally refusing entrance to black students and Justice Department officials. President John F. Kennedy then federalizes the Alabama National Guard, and Governor Wallace removes himself from blocking the entrance of the Negro students.

1963 *(continued)*

June 12. Medgar Evers, NAACP leader in Jackson, Mississippi, is assassinated in the early-morning darkness by a rifle bullet, at his home. His memorial service is held in Jackson on June 15, and he is buried in Arlington National Cemetery, Washington, D.C., on June 19. Byron de la Beckwith is finally indicted and found guilty of the murder in 1994.

August 28. The March on Washington, the first large integrated protest march, is held in Washington, D.C. Dr. King and other civil rights leaders meet with President John F. Kennedy in the White House, and afterward, Dr. King delivers his "I Have a Dream" speech on the steps of the Lincoln Memorial.

September. Dr. King's book *Strength to Love* is published by Harper & Row.

September 2–10. Governor Wallace orders the Alabama state troopers to stop the court-ordered integration of Alabama's elementary and high schools until he is enjoined by court injunction from doing so. By September 10, specific schools are actually integrated by court order.

November 22. President Kennedy is assassinated in Dallas, Texas.

1964

1964

Summer. COFO (Council of Federated Organizations) initiates the Mississippi Summer Project, a voter-registration drive organized and run by black and white students.

May–June. Dr. King joins other SCLC workers in demonstrations for the integration of public accommodations in St. Augustine, Florida. He is jailed.

June. Dr. King's book *Why We Can't Wait* is published by Harper & Row.

June 21. Three civil rights workers—James Chaney (black) and Andrew Goodman and Michael Schwerner (white)—are reported missing after a short trip to Philadelphia, Mississippi.

July 2. Dr. King attends the signing of the public accommodations bill, part of the Civil Rights Act of 1964, by President Lyndon B. Johnson in the White House.

July 18–23. Riots occur in Harlem. One black man is killed.

August 4. The bodies of civil rights workers James Chaney, Andrew Goodman, and Michael Schwerner are discovered by FBI agents buried near the town of Philadelphia, Mississippi. Neshoba County sheriff Rainey and his deputy, Cecil Price, are allegedly implicated in the murders.

August. Riots occur in New Jersey, Illinois, and Pennsylvania.

September. Dr. King and the Reverend Ralph Abernathy visit West Berlin at the invitation of Mayor Willy Brandt.

September 18. Dr. King has an audience with Pope Paul VI at the Vatican.

1964 *(continued)*

1965

1966

December 10. Dr. King receives the Nobel Peace Prize in Oslo, Norway.

1965

February 21. Malcolm X, leader of the Organization of Afro-American Unity and former Black Muslim leader, is murdered by blacks in New York City.

March 7. A group of marching demonstrators (from SNCC and SCLC) led by SCLC's Hosea Williams are beaten by state highway patrolmen (under the direction of Al Lingo) and sheriff's deputies (under the leadership of Jim Clark) when attempting to march across the Edmund Pettus Bridge on their planned march to Montgomery, Alabama, from Selma, Alabama. An order by Governor Wallace had prohibited the march.

March 9. James Reeb, a white Unitarian minister, is beaten by four segregationists in Selma and dies two days later.

March 15. President Johnson addresses the nation and Congress. He describes the voting rights bill he will submit to Congress in two days and uses the slogan of the civil rights movement, "We Shall Overcome."

March 16. Black and white demonstrators are beaten by sheriff's deputies and police on horseback in Montgomery.

March 21–25. Over three thousand protest marchers leave Selma for a march to Montgomery, protected by federal troops. They are joined along the way by a total of twenty-five thousand marchers. Upon reaching the capitol building they hear an address by Dr. King.

March 25. Viola Liuzzo, wife of a Detroit Teamsters Union business agent, is shot and killed while driving a carload of marchers back to Selma.

July. Dr. King visits Chicago. SCLC joins with the Coordinating Council of Community Organizations (CCCO), led by Al Raby, in the Chicago Project.

August–December. In Alabama, SCLC spearheads voter registration campaigns in Greene and Wilcox counties and in the cites of Montgomery and Birmingham.

August 6. The 1965 Voting Rights Act is signed by President Johnson.

August 11–16. In Watts, the black ghetto of Los Angeles, riots leave thirty-five dead, of whom twenty-eight are black.

1966

February. Dr. King rents an apartment in the black ghetto of Chicago.

February 23. Dr. King meets with Elijah Muhammad, leader of the Black Muslims, in Chicago.

March. Dr. King takes over a Chicago slum building and is sued by its owner.

1966 *(continued)*

March 25. The Supreme Court rules any poll tax unconstitutional.

Spring. Dr. King makes a tour of Alabama to help elect black candidates. The Albany primary is held, the first time since Reconstruction that blacks have voted in any numbers.

May 16. An antiwar statement by Dr. King is read at a large Washington rally to protest the war in Vietnam. Dr. King agrees to serve as cochairman of Clergy and Laymen Concerned About Vietnam (CLCV).

June. Stokely Carmichael and Willie Ricks (SNCC) use the slogan "Black Power" in public for the first time before reporters in Greenwood, Mississippi.

June 6. James Meredith is shot soon after beginning his 220-mile "March Against Fear" from Memphis, Tennessee, to Jackson, Mississippi.

July 10. Dr. King launches a drive to make Chicago an "open city" in regard to housing.

August 5. Dr. King is stoned in Chicago as he leads a march through crowds of angry whites in the Gage Park section of Chicago's southwest side.

September. SCLC launches a project with the aim of integrating schools in Grenada, Mississippi.

Fall. SCLC initiates the Alabama Citizen Education Project in Wilcox County.

1967

1967

January. Dr. King writes his book *Where Do We Go from Here?* while in Jamaica.

March 12. Alabama is ordered to desegregate all public schools.

March 25. Dr. King attacks the government's Vietnam policy in a speech at the Chicago Coliseum.

May 10–11. One black student is killed in a riot on the campus of all-Negro Jackson State College, Jackson, Mississippi.

July 6. The Justice Department reports that more than 50 percent of all eligible black voters are registered in Mississippi, Georgia, Alabama, Louisiana, and South Carolina.

July 12–17. Twenty-three people die and 725 are injured in riots in Newark, New Jersey.

July 23–30. Forty-three die and 324 are injured in the Detroit riots, the worst of the century.

July 26. Black leaders—Martin Luther King, Jr., A. Philip Randolph, Roy Wilkins, and Whitney Young—appeal for an end to the riots, "which have proved ineffective and damaging to the civil rights cause and the entire nation."

1967 *(continued)*

October 30. The Supreme Court upholds the contempt-of-court convictions of Dr. King and seven other black leaders who led 1963 marches in Birmingham. Dr. King and his aides enter jail to serve four-day sentences.

November 27. Dr. King announces the formation by SCLC of a Poor People's Campaign, with the aim of representing the problems of poor blacks and whites.

1968

1968

February 12. Sanitation workers strike in Memphis, Tennessee.

March 28. Dr. King leads six thousand protesters on a march through downtown Memphis in support of striking sanitation workers. Disorder breaks out, during which black youths loot stores. One sixteen-year-old is killed, fifty persons are injured.

April 3. Dr. King's last speech, entitled, "I've Been to the Mountain Top," is delivered at the Memphis Masonic temple.

Martin Luther King, Jr., is assasinated.

April 4. Dr. King is assassinated by a sniper as he stands talking on the balcony of his second-floor room at the Lorraine Motel in Memphis. He dies in St. Joseph's Hospital from a gunshot wound in the neck. James Earl Ray is later captured and convicted of the murder.

June 5. Presidential candidate Senator Robert Kennedy is shot in Los Angeles. He dies the next day.